The Roads

DAVID KENNEDY was born in Leicester in 1959. He co-edited *The New Poetry* and is the author of *New Relations: The Refashioning of British Poetry 1980–1994*. He edited the magazine of innovative poetry and poetics *The Paper* from 2000 to 2004 and publishes widely on contemporary British and Irish poetry. His publications include *The President of Earth: New and Selected Poems*; *The Dice Cup*, translations of Max Jacob's prose poems with Christopher Pilling; and the collaboration *Eight Excursions* with Rupert Loydell. Monographs on Douglas Dunn and on elegy are forthcoming, respectively, in the Northcote House series Writers and Their Work and in Routledge's New Critical Idiom. David lives in Sheffield with his wife Christine.

Books by David Kennedy

Books of Poetry
The Elephant's Typewriter (1996)
Men's Talk (1998)
Cities (1998)
Four True Prophecies of the New State (1999)
The Fiery Chariot (2000)
Max Jacob: The Dice Cup Part I (translation with Christopher Pilling, 2000)
Cornell: A Circuition Around His Circumambulation (2001)
The President of Earth: New and Selected Poems (2002)
Eight Excursions (collaboration with Rupert Loydell, 2003)

Books About Poetry
New Relations: The Refashioning of British Poetry 1980–1994 (1996)

As Editor
The New Poetry with Michael Hulse and David Morley (1993)
Additional Apparitions: Poetry, Performance & Site Specificity with Keith Tuma (2002)

The Roads

David Kennedy

SALT

CAMBRIDGE

PUBLISHED BY SALT PUBLISHING
PO Box 937, Great Wilbraham, Cambridge PDO CB1 5JX United Kingdom
PO Box 202, Applecross, Western Australia 6153

First published 2004

Printed and bound in the United Kingdom by Lightning Source

Typeset in Swift 9.5 / 13

ISBN 1 84471 107 2 paperback

SP

1 3 5 7 9 8 6 4 2

To Betty, Christine and Marion

Contents

THE ROADS   1
The Enchanted Lake   3
Red Horse   4
Poem with Hand and Small Fish   5
The Roads   6
Warsaw Nights   10
Balloon : Fig   11
A Rare Part of History   12
Another Moment: A Georgic on the Eve of the
    Invasion of Iraq, 30 March 2003   13
666 FM   14
Indoors   17
This Is Korea   18
Walking Book   20
553 Steps Around Auzon   23
Minster   30
The Opposite of Writing   34
The Haunting   35
Words   36
The Process of Language   37
The Preservation of Light   41
On Reading John Kinsella's Peripheral Light   43
Rehearsing Two of Ric Caddel's '5 Career Moves . . .'
    for a Reading   45
Schiele Sprechgesang   46
Lucky Garden Night Blues   48
from The Book of Roads   51
Dhromi: The Roads   52

THE GRAVES   55
Dr. Kennedy's Country Dream   57
Books of the Dead   58
At Anton Walbrook's Grave   61
My Father's Deaths   64
Egyptian Elegy for My Father   66
Alum Raptures   71
Six Staves for Koch's Grave   74
Postcards of Penthesilea   77
Poem Begun in a Small Notebook   82
Call & Response   85
History of the Woe   86

THE LARKS   87
Advice To All Girls In Love   89
Bohemian Fantasy   90
Chef in the Dusk   91
Found on a Flipchart   92
Fabula Rasa   93
Ink Tunes   94
Art Texts — 1   95
Lament of the River   96
My Dream Tom Raworth's Oklahoma Windows   97
My Dream Alan Halsey's Sentences Cool Down   98
My Dream Frances Presley Delivers A Book   99
My Dream Picasso Shows Me The Secret   100
Myth in Samoa   101
Poem   102
Art Texts — 2   103
Symphonie Fantastique   104
Teach Yourself Criticism: The Texas Poetry Examiner   105

The Return of the Art of Poetry 106
The Wild Anger is Tired of Soap 107
What To Eat in Poland, or, We Say What We See 108
When I Was Spanish 109
Word Girl 111
Art Texts — 3 112

CORNELL: A CIRCUITION AROUND HIS CIRCUMAMBULATION 113

Notes 129

Acknowledgements

Acknowledgements are due to the editors of the following publications in which some of these poems first appeared:

Echolocation, Filling Station, Fulcrum, GutCult, Jacket, Muse Apprentice Guild, Samizdat, Stride, The Paper and *The Wide Skirt*.

'A Rare Part of History' first appeared in *Eight Excursions*, a collaboration with Rupert Loydell, published by The Cherry On The Top Press in 2003.

An earlier version of 'Cornell: A Circuition Around His Circumambulation' was made and published in November 2000 in a signed, limited handmade edition for the London Artists' Book Fair by The Cherry On The Top Press; and then published by West House Books in an edition of 200 copies in 2001.

'553 Steps Around Auzon' was first published by The Cherry On The Top Press in 2004 as a limited edition artist's book with photographs by Christine Kennedy. A French edition, translated by Anne-Marie Comtour, will be published in 2005. The text was originally written in response to a commission from the late Ian Robinson in 2003 and is dedicated to his memory.

'Rehearsing Two of Ric Caddel's "5 Career Moves" for a Reading' was first published in *Onsets—A Breviary (Synopticon?) of Poems 13 Lines or Under*, edited by Nate Dorward and published by *The Gig* for the occasion of the Toronto Small-Press Bookfair, Spring 2004.

'Dhromi: The Roads' was commended by the judges of the Arvon International Poetry Competition 2004 and first published in *The Arvon International Poetry Competition Anthology 2004*.

'Dr Kennedy's Country Dream' was broadcast on BBC Radio 3's *The Verb*, 13 November 2004.

'Poem with Hand and Small Fish' was first published in *The Ring of Words: Poems from The Daily Telegraph Arvon International Poetry Competition 1998*.

The completion of *The Roads* has been made possible by a Grant for the Arts from Arts Council England (Yorkshire).

The Roads

The Enchanted Lake

Beautiful young violinists of the student orchestra,
how you make me lick my lips
as I am carried over the audience
on the crest of your unsalted concentration!
You take me to the end of the concert
and let me watch you singing your violins to sleep
in their little coffins.
You let me see that sometimes the velvet is red
and sometimes the velvet is blue.
You take me high above the city
to the end of the night
and show me bachelors, young and old,
in their crusty flats, nodding
over their catalogues of dead flies and stiff socks
as they dream of savouring
long warm draughts of your bathwater.
We leave them to watch the spiders
in the first, empty light of dawn
getting their webs ready for the day's business.
At last, you take me to the beginning of music.
I am so small I could be swaddled in one page of the score.
My mother's face is very big.
She lifts me on to her shoulder
and, moving her hand back and forth,
back and forth over my tiny spine,
sings a song about an enchanted lake.

Red Horse

In the town by the wide river
all the lovers are asleep.
Their dreams rise up chimneys
and emerge, distending slowly
like inverted drops of water,
then expanding to their full size
and falling upwards.
Up, up they float until the earth
begins to curve beneath them;
up, up where the moon hangs off a rack
at the top of night's big shed
watching the small hours fossick
and scurry furtively between deep blue shadows
on the banks of the wide river.
What big dreams some people have,
the moon thinks, and what strange ones!
What is a unicorn doing
with all that flat pack furniture?
And whose granny is that
going into a wardrobe with Stalin
and coming out again with a bag of mushrooms?
The dream that pops out
of our chimney is about a red horse.
Red horse, where are you taking us, red horse,
on your back as wide as the wide river?
The stars tinkle in his bridle
as he tosses his head and neighs a giant horsey laugh.
His teeth are lighted windows in the night.
He carries us, sleeping, on his back until morning.

Poem with Hand and Small Fish

This is the poem that begins by understanding love.
Just like that? Yes, just 'like that'. Look: a hand resting in
marbling green waters with little fish playing through
its fingers, giving it otherwise unavailable micro-services,

things it never knew it wanted until it got them
—just like this year and its new saloons or the world
and the Mona Lisa. Upstairs in the lodging house,
there is rhythmic banging from one of the attic rooms

as, tears streaming down his face, the old man works
     with mallets
an elephant's typewriter which prints 'Fifi'
and the word 'idiot' for the trainer's name.
Later, he will serenade his life with 'The Isle of Capri'

played on a brass sousaphone. Old Mrs. Czerkas,
the landlady, is deaf to all complaints because she, too,
understands love as this poem does as it ends with a donkey
—practical, sad, surreal, susceptible to rescue.

The Roads

for John Hartley Williams

The roads yearn
in the sunlight
before sloping off
into the forest
and their verges hum
with flowers
like young brides
on wedding mornings.

Under the trees
where the low walls
of dead fields
dodder and totter
into moss and brambles
a bridle jingles once:
a black mare waits
and an open carriage.

Your own desires
whisper in the leaves,
in the long grasses
pulling your foot to the step.
As you sit, a blanket
flows up over your legs
like Granny tucking you in
after a bad dream.

Deep into the forest
trots the mare.
You do not hear dead branches
snapping at the spokes
of the wheels.
You do not see the light
grow thin and frigid
—you are dreaming

of the roads, the roads.
The crests of gentle cambers
or thick, buttery mud
—it's all the same
to your young man's boots!
But all your dreaming
returns to the same scene:
your mother and your sisters

spilling from the doorway
of the cottage, begging
you to stay at home
with the cows and chickens.
When you next awake
the trees are the thin stalks
of green iron lampposts
with creeper picked out in gold

and four branches
holding lamps like teardrops.
The roads are lined
with pavement cafés
whose gorgeous waitresses
speak inside your head.
To everything they say
you answer 'yes'.

After rich cake
and jugs of sweet wine
that fills your veins
like syrup distilled
from sleep
you need the restroom.
Pushing open the only door
at the back you step out

under the trees.
The gorgeous waitresses
sit on the grass
in twos and threes.
They file each other's perfect teeth
to points like needles.
And as they work they sing
the old song that frightens children:

Young man, young man,
how long have you been away?
The village has no sons left.
Your mother does
what all mothers do there,
sits crying in the great circle.
Your Granny looks at the violets
from underneath.

Young man, young man,
how long have you been hanging
from the rafters of the forest?
How long has your husk
whispered there?

Warsaw Nights
for Jacek Gutorow & Jerzy Jarniewicz

The last stroke of midnight clangs
in the phone. It's the front desk:
the boat you ordered is waiting.
You forgot that 'perhaps'
sounds exactly like 'sea'
when they asked if you were going out.
The sails fill slowly like rose petals
falling through honey
and the boat slides on butter
the moon spreads over the empty squares
and their uninhabited plinths.
Where are all the poets and heroes?
Down in the red cellar
standing you drink after drink.
Everyone's getting excited
about poetry and history,
taking it in turns
to hold forth like film directors
addressing their casts.
You feel you should speak too,
bring together the remotest things
on a hairpin bend
in the conversation or coin a bon mot
like 'A new century is crackling in the hearth'.
But what do you know,
what can you say about history?
The pork escalope they serve you
has been bashed into the shape
of a pig's ear that rings
with its own dying squeal.

Balloon : Fig

I can hardly hear myself think
over the gasps and gusts of a balloon
rising up the burning blue evening.
There is something I want to say about desire
that's to do with the wisps of hair escaping
your French pleat—if only you'd keep your head still!
And, anyway, according to you it's your turn.

First, you show me the insides of a fig,
its flesh made of eyes on stalks.
It is horrible but I must look in.
It seems to be mine already.
Then, you guide my fingers
into broad beans; together we rifle
their moist silky purses to push out blind pearls.

A Rare Part of History

The past streams off us into the future
and when it's all gone
we will be what we were again—nothing.
In the arts centre, it's 1975.
Different lifts go to odd
and even floors and the carpets
are psychedelic ice floes
beginning to break up in early spring.
Somehow we've made it
to hear the old poet mumbling through
his once-in-a-decade reading.
He doesn't want to be here
because he's been where it's at and it wasn't here.
The audience is old people
who haven't been out since 1969
and young people who wish they could look like that
without the same effort of self-denial.
The old people think where it's at
is wherever the old poet is
but since the old poet doesn't want to be
wherever he's supposed to be,
where it's at is always already somewhere else.
And the old poet says, "The instruction
0x77f52004 is an application error
and is better half-remembered".
And the oldest members of the audience answer,
"The referenced memory
0x007f4f10 could not be written".
So this is a rare part of history
where everyone goes home happy.

Another Moment: A Georgic on the Eve of the Invasion of Iraq, 30 March 2003

Spring corroborates
our assumptions
with evidence
we hardly examine:
trees' armatures
blurry with new leaf,
familiar sequences
of snowdrop and crocus.
Like any act
of reading, we scan
for a general sense
we're happy with.
Let me tell you
this is how we let
substance get lost
in process.
Thirty-six days now
without rain here
as unnoticed
as eleven days
with truths so general
they've mutated
into something useless.
Amongst silent majorities
of daffodils: dandelions,
the odd buttercup
a whole month early;
more examples of shifts
we live inside so can't see
happening in front of us.

666 FM

Guitar runs spill all over the brown rice belt
from sash windows that rise and fall like guillotines.
Citizen passing by, sooty pedestrian, tarnished republican,
I take whatever I think it is they offer me
as a respite from my own temporary indentations
in the class system where even the smallest change
gets handled as sheets of heavy gauge white card,
double imperial size, in a gale
that fills the pavements with jangles of litter
fervent to enlist in the war of the player-pianos.
So it's not the season for the famine of the wind
to bring out the flapping scarecrow in people
—everyone's on the look out for thermals
to give them an easy ride on the gluey ooze
of August's marmalade through the yards and ginnels,
knots and mazes of the city's self-constricting brief—
but the streets can still exile anyone from hope
when the hope was for an emptying meditation
and the day's observing eye's found unscientific.
Bees crawl into flowers, change the frequency,
and the devil's voice comes out,
the teased screech, torn yowl
of ripped metal tuned just off station.
There are so many things I don't know belong to me
whirling me closer and closer to the plughole
of a demented kabuki burlesque
I'm almost ready to believe I *can* be reconstituted
by the nightly parables of disorder and control,
how clean is your friendly bacteria sunshine grime swap,
before going to bed, failing to sleep,
failing to sleep, failing to sleep,
and hearing the city bang bang bang
in my chest all night.

The sirens wailing in my lungs
say there are so many things I don't know belong to me
that I want to wail back I don't want what I know
so anything that dilutes the grief
of finding oneself in the story of machines
can start to feel like a fulcrum
for lifting the miseries of choice.
Intermittent pips of wind chimes drip
into my head as if inanity as poignant sophistication
or absurd nakedness as sublime humanity
were policies to win an election with
but then, from ledge to ledge, from tree
to choking tree, the birdsong starts up again:
'Unless it pays it goes—unless it pays it goes.'
'It goes it goes it goes.' 'It goes—unless it pays.'
And I just can't get you out of my head,
dream in which I wake up in my old philosophy class.
The subject is the acquisition of knowledge
and we have an hour to write an essay.
We each have an answer booklet
and our starting point, in cold print,
is exactly what each of us said when we came in
followed by 'analyse', 'justify' or 'relate'.
My words were a greeting to an old friend,
who must be having the same dream,
"All right Havelda, all right?"
I panic to the teacher on his dais,
one of those fierce mid-twentieth century bachelors
with the look of Wittgenstein
who swivels in his captain's chair
south-east south-west south-south-east.
He puts down his volume of Loeb's Classical Library,
leans out from the flying buttresses

of his world heritage site four-piece suit
and says "Don't worry, there are rooms and rooms,
corridors and corridors, and in some town or another
at least one dog who knows why he barks."

Indoors

The moralists are back,
cruising heaven in their patched
and wheezing balloons
or winding themselves over our cities
in their cable cars and rusty buckets,
peering peevishly this way
and that through opera glasses.

The year dithers. It's the month
of something to do with interest rates,
a fine time to tell me you think
the destiny of our love
is like a 500ft superstack designed
so toxic emissions blow into the next state.
I preferred it when you were a bridge

and I was something atomized and flung
from your cables. I'm better off indoors
with the phone's comforting mockery
of something organic,
my young tom running in
all cheerful and shiny
like a new top hat.

This Is Korea

Down the expressway from Pusan, south-west
    To Nam-Hae Island and the sea,
The ebb-chink-shift-surge rhythm of the tolls
    And white gloves cradling carbines
Stop our music bursting the car
        When the singer yells
"I call her by her family name"
           —And, you know, he better
Because, after all, this is Korea
Where people respect people terrifically.

We like this mix, all strophe and antistrophe:
    The coastal plain carbuncled
With wooded hills and, in between, patches
    Of pastel concrete acne,
A country scratching itself hard
        As it lies half-asleep
In the horizon's scroll painting dream
        Of icing-sugared peaks.
It's a sweet dream that catches us too:
We see the roadsigns for 'Foggy Area'

Only as we're cutting through clotted air,
    Heavy swags and bolts of mist,
Making our exit and breaking out
    Into tall, cut glass sunlight.
Everywhere is paddy-fields,
        High-rise lily pads
Or multi-storey golf tees shelving
        Up and down, down and up.
We saw plump pumpkins, watermelons,
Piled up on the verge and road gangs in straw hats

And flip-flops patching up the potholes
                    But the best thing there
Was a sensuous dog, a beautiful cool dog
                    Walking through the morning.

Walking Book
for Stephen Vincent

I

                  stutter up
        steep shingle
           uttered in
                      crunchy syllables
           rewind
        and slip
      steps thaw
               the shingle
        steps thaw
     and run
(all the way back to the car)
into ways of walking
                 step by step
        steps
      stutter and
lurch through
the brightness of walking

II

                  stammer
    and jump
        through the maze
of a rocky bed

    dead ends of walking
indistinctly visible
            step
      by
step

III

through little plants
and run into the floor

of a   little
     twisty   stream

immense river of walking
in a twisty little stream

IV

faded scores
worn needlecord
of strip lynchets

wet-paper-dried rumples

the cracked spines
                    of the hollows
hollows
          syncline
and
     anticline
then
     along   seacombe bottom

to stacked shelves
of grey stone

shale pastry

book of steps

                    up
clamber

pages all about
us too heavy
to open
                    to turn

                    up
clamber

                    to watch the sea
        lathering
one edge of the floor

553 Steps Around Auzon

Once upon a time, lèro, lèro, lèro,
two streams carved a spine.

(Who sings in the earth before
first light shows through?)

L'Auzon et le Gauderel,
au pied du Haut-Pays.

(Robert in his cellar
is nursing his *jus*)

Then, to the east, narrowed it
to a spur, lèro dèrèro.

(I was off to the high woods
to see my love true)

Below the plinth of the forest,
le Gauderel et l'Auzon.

(When he bade me step down
and drink glasses two)

The spur above the cereal plain,
baïlèro lô.

(Who hears Robert singing
beware of his brew)

The spur in an open casket
of verdure.

(O Robert, naughty Robert,
it passes straight through)

Lives clung to the granite until,
ti lirou, stone became town.

(The moon it will sail
'fore my love I do see)

'Edge' into 'ledge'
and 'terre' into 'terrasse'.

(Two glasses with Robert
make me stop at each tree)

A short night lifts on acid trees splashing green smoking blue up the sheer spur holding the Romanesque church up to the light. Choked shelves at the spur's turn were, legend has it, hanging gardens once. Three pumpkins, *trois potirons*, on a low wall rest red arses. Ellipsis at the end or the start of the next bit.

We are what stone never dreamt and cannot see but witnesses everywhere our belatedness. Stone's only dream is stone, stone: stone coming back through soil, run-off turning paths to sluices. Stone's lesson is restless shifting from foothold to foothold. Luck is having a perch.

The sunburnt serpent wants to bite through this old double-door but he keeps getting delayed. Every time he opens his jaws a new self pops out, so fast and so often he doesn't seem to be moving at all. If he could just get it right and sink fangs into wood, the twelve fur-suited dolls standing to attention, six on each door, would spring into action—except they've been waiting so long their heads have dropped off and they wouldn't know what to do. What will happen if the serpent succeeds! But after all, the whole thing's only twelve deer's feet nailed up on washed out wooden doors. A bizarre twelve-line concrete poem, *douzain concret*, over a rusty old latch.

Between two houses, Rue Longue: ivy pentecost, glossolalia, frenzied lentil throat of stones dissociating in Lenten frost and blaze d'août. So long as virtu goes on piling debris, history as faith in neglect's what the scene espouses.

Vallée de l'Allier. No lullay lullaby, vallée de l'Allier, in epic scarps, tossed steeps, that worry sleep with dreams of clambering up to try to climb down to or from towns paved and floored with riverbed pebbles. These fallen steps, moth-eaten bolts of moss pinned with weeds, holding geranium pots: shrine to walking's graft.

Through night's shredded sack, moon's pitted bone. The town bottomless. Remembering the old tale where the amorous priest, off to the villein's wife, through *grant meschaance* fell in a ditch with a wolf, streets become pits; alleys open trapdoors. The disused terraces below the castle would be good to stand with a white guitar, loon banjo, strike single strings and raise a voice, like the owl's, concealed but threaded here.

Minster
for Richard Burdett, Alan Halsey and Geraldine Monk

AN ENTRING

At
Beverley. Byland.
Fountains. Hexham.
Howden. Kilton.
Rievaulx.

Found
Two birds, poss. cockerels.
Fishes. Harps.

Untidy crosses. Stars. Scratch geometry.

Arrows, sometimes w/o feathers. Spears.

At
        Ripon.
Roche. Sandal.
Sherburn-in-Elmet. Skelton.
Southwell. York.

I

In the thick
of mark: murk
of trace.

On Roche's
soffit, Hexham's
facet.

Signal opacity
count readings.

II

Men stir
terms in
inert ms.

III

The Master.
The use of the men.
The intention of a stone to one corner.
Fissure.
The floor below.
Written sight.
The shadowy figure.
The chisel.

IV

The stone
folded together
leads into
the chisel.

V

There is fed by the chisel

        murmuring → ↑ ↑ ×

The book of sight

        skill marks bellowing above our ears

VI

The chisel could
read

The master would
know

        the murk
of the men

VII

At least
one fish
stands on
its tail.

VIII

Keys on the wall

Scroll up
and down the body
of their murky light

An astounding flurry
full of their career

The wall is locked

IX

Minster

Smite
        Mitre

Sawn stone soars
on written sight

        Inter
Insert

Termin_s

The Opposite of Writing

what is the opposite of writing what is the opposite of writing what is the opposite of writing what is the opposite of writing what is the opposite writing what is writing the opposite what is the opposite is the opposite already writing

The Haunting

At the end
of the movie

the survivors crawl
to safety through

a hole in
language

Words

Words,
half-chewed,

half-prepared,
fall onto

the floor where,
sticky,

they get hairy.
Back in our mouths

they would choke us
like furballs.

I do not want
to cook with them.

The Process of Language
to Christine

flux mother

la mer de ma mère
la mère de ma mer

    pulse mother

   ∽

grains of sound
spindrift la mer
de ma mère

   I

Vous voulez faire écrivain?
Choose your genre,
find your position in the field.

Vous voulez faire de la littérature?
Strike a key. Don't worry
if you have to press the key "esc".

   ∽

Now I am sending you
some orientations.

First of all, with the key
"esc" you stop; then

it is necessary
to start again.

   ∽

Vous voulez faire écrivain?
Tap the language.
The needle should
move in the field
of the father's say so.

～

Now I am sending you
some mirrors.

First of all, with the key
'history' you happen; then

it is necessary
to escape again.

These are the returns
I have noticed to let you know.

～

The nature of desire.
Ideas of thee return.

～

Vous voulez faire écrivain?
What are you afraid of?
The nature of desire.

II

I was late
talking my mother
says I was
late walking my
mother says
but once
you went you
never fell over
and once you
started you
never stopped

~

mother lend me
your mirror
I will keep it
dusty mother
lend me emergence
in speckulation

~

Do you remember,
mother, the game
we played with
grains of sound?
Played it just
the once, mother.
I was with
you, mother, but
I don't remember.

~

mother lend me
your mirror
I will keep it
dusty mother
I will value
inability to come
into focus

~

Do you remember
the grains, mother?
I have drained
my cup, mother.
Please read it.

III

a trench dug
in the field
of the father
finds crumbs,
tesserae

~

being
is nearly all
ebbing

The Preservation of Light

My father said, You do not have to answer a question.
Light is a question, my father said.

The bridge sings its own song back to itself
over tough little plants spurting

into the rocks on the dry stream bed;
and his words come back to me,

said by another bridge in a colder place.
My father was a painter; it was his habit

to point such things out, to attend to them.
Walnut and carob drop their smooth mouldings

of protein and sugar on the stony soil
round the abandoned chapel

where, once a year, a priest comes
and says mass to keep it holy.

The tentative notes
of a goat bell are a weak memory

or prediction of his coming; and their tone,
which says there is no empty space,

no finally determined gesture,
is the only way of measuring

the long, open textures of the afternoon.
Then the view drops away

into the rough, stubbly valley
and different questions of light

which lead the eye up to a blurred gap
with shadows coming and going

like movements behind gauze.
This is the sea and the islands in it

boiling in the late sun.
I imagine the priest visiting each one,

standing by similar chapels,
watching each stone give its answers

to the light while loops of goat music
cycle through extended intervals;

then checking it off on the list
of things God wants keeping.

On Reading John Kinsella's *Peripheral Light*

I

To wake up
sharpened, like Smithson was,
  to a sense of rust
as a fundamental
  property
of steel means registering
  our presence
here as care and neglect
  twisted and
folded into one edge,

  one surface;
feeling words and poems
  as oxides,
as mode distressing mode.
  Convolvulus
graphs it, or something close,
  in wire mesh,
and brambles too, their raw lines
  snagged on plot
and overgrowth alike.

II

What frost bit,
sun warped and hand left,
  the wind pries
and the back comes off
  pastoral:
big valves turn out to be
  the tanks
and silos dominating
  real lives,
coding generations.

It's like this:
out on wheatlands wide stage
   in the shade
of a corrugated
   cylinder
Florizel is praising
   Perdita
who's matching invoices,
   earpiece in
for market news, weather.

Rehearsing Two of Ric Caddel's '5 Career Moves . . .' for a Reading

Thought, our daily work, in a short set.
Handmade textures, single
and perfect, signed and beating
with swells and breaks, bars our

season's written over. Melody
we make in making it,
perpetually mid-phrase out
of the low hum of us,

the wash of our traffic. Breath's sounded out
—our start and stop, question and
answer—and then happily released
to join the dots, one, two, three.

Schiele Sprechgesang

Bodies
all one
body.
Drastic
gists. Snapped
I's. Vertical
rifts. Naked
wolf-selves,
unsocial-
ized limbs.
Sex gang
crime scene
sprechgesang.
Prick
bodies.
Crack
mouths.
Gash
and wang.
Botched
make-up,
flowers
of souls' slang,
bashes presence
from appearance.
In canvas cells,
yob octaves'
enamel
blotches
clang
and drang
on world

as body,
on body
as stick
to poke
death with.
The century
grew into
these bodies.

Lucky Garden Night Blues

I woke up this morning and something about the way you had scratched both sides of every record in my collection of two hundred and forty seven not especially rare but mostly irreplaceable because not on CD modern jazz LPs confirmed my suspicions that the publicity brochure of our love was certainly not alerting anyone that we were Europe's largest manufacturer of kitchen knives and housewares whose flagship brand sold over 50 million units worldwide in its first ten years and whose remarkable success and growth rate are based on a unique key strategy combining customer service, product development and process automation. No, no one could say of us, all phone calls answered in three rings and all enquiries answered the same day which I guess is why you left me these records as evidence. My first thought was to throw them all away but then since you were clearly bequeathing me a choice between, amongst other things, poise and disintegration, I thought about having myself photographed burning them all on some prominence and sending you a large format print as evidence of a different order, as evidence, in fact, of a rather triumphant location of the two choices in each other. It seems to me now, after the dust stirred up by taking each LP from its sleeve to see if you had scratched it and then re-sleeving it has settled, that since the most remarkable thing about the records is that although no two scratches are alike all scratches are conveying the same message, they should be exhibited somewhere, sleeveless, because there really is something about a sleeveless record, hung surreally like two hundred and forty seven black hats in rows on a cool green wall and with a sad and mysterious title like *The Art of Love* or *The Book of the Courtier* or *Hey! Just A Minute I'm Talking* or *You Never Let Me Finish*, in plain sight of those who will meet again Friday in *The Undefended Heart* and then after closing time move on somewhere like *The Maudlin Disaster* where they will finish around two by pooling their last piastres to pour a libation to 'the one' who did not appear again tonight.

Yes, I woke up this morning in a novel that nobody wants to rent and reading through the blurb of our love again over melancholy coffee the colour of a river where, in the shadow of a bridge, a big nameless fish floats up, noses the water's petrolized skin without breaking the surface, and returns to age-cold darkness, I had to say that I agreed with you that it read like something out of last week's paper, not one of the usual sweet lullabies that keep the town asleep like 'Ambitious unveiled thriving community space consultants multi-million chance' or '£2 million revealed capacity luxurious rivals capital Olympic', more like the interview with the Chief Constable in last week's paper where he was talking about duelling and said that "The suppression of this absorbing activity has created a need for so many compensatory pastimes, comparable in violence, however lamentably inferior in style". Yes, I had to admit that there had never been any chance of us sitting in brasseries along the river, where they're building a series of replicas of Nero's city-sized palace, sitting like young men with listings who can't wait for morning to finish polishing the waves giving themselves starring roles in mini-sagas called *Power Breakfast* and *Getting Paid* because we were just that bit too old to have wooed one another with brand names in the first place so there was no point in even pretending to lament the non-existent promise of youth with 'wear by' labels in one's clothes, the will to heroism deflected into 'the product promise' and knowing nothing but the camp classicism of a comic opera.

No, reading through the blurb of our love again, it was clear we were never going to have headed paper and a fleet of vans sloganized with "From mortuaries to saunas—we get everywhere" but, most depressingly, I couldn't even find any of the phrases I really like such as, in a French accent, "I come to you naked, without knowledge. I have left all my black polo neck sweaters behind in the cafés of irony and won't be going back for them. You must teach me to understand vegetables and to feel the wind on my skin again." Instead, I read "Aspires to discontinuous narrative, stories entire in themselves but each developing the preoccupations of the others and therefore compounding the common protagonist's distress." So, you're right, I wouldn't want to buy that and I couldn't believe in it enough to try and sell it either. And now it's been dark for a while and the moon is anodizing the town, covering everything in a satin aluminium finish and sooner or later the town will blanche and go sick outside *The Lucky Garden* takeaway—motto: enjoy life eat here often. And now I've got the dust of so many cities on my feet and no hands to wash it off but my o-o-own.

from The Book of Roads

Empty roads between evergreens in the early late light of a November 2 p.m. have the unmistakable quality of the long Finland you cross between open-air tango pavilions in quiet agricultural towns. You take the floor as the descending minor melodies and slow 'lazy triplet' tempi bring out the first sullen stars. Later, when night is shot full of them, you will be the one singing 'Give Me Just One Word' and 'Once I Waited For Someone'.

≈

I left early to beat the traffic. The roads of my town were waiting for the resinous scrape of a cello cadenza. The motorways were a perfect communication in which I was neither subject nor object. I returned late in beaten traffic. I crawled through the inept innuendoes of the machines: Escort, Lexus, Volvo.

≈

Here are some warning signs we have in my country. A grand piano. A sleeping cat. A leaping dolphin. A line of washing blowing left. A line of washing blowing right. Wind chimes. A bachelor. A man carrying a large fish.

Dhromi: The Roads

Under the Tree of Idleness
in the square outside the main taverna,
a small pride of dazed men stirred and stretched
as though moving cost them a small fortune,
and a fat moth whirred out of the leaves.

There was a festival in Spili
and the Bishop was in residence.
As we came into town,
dusk sprinkling the air with the ashes of the day,
his windows burned high on the scrubby hillside.
In the tombs and shrines candles flickered
as if the dead were about to get up
and go about their business
with the rest of the town rattled awake
by the screech and yowl of the carpenter's shop
ripping wood for wardrobe doors.
We looked into its bright mouth
and saw a row of gaping cabinets
leant against the wall like coffins for giants.

We spent the hour round nightfall
by the Turkish fountain,
counting its nineteen lion's heads,
wondering at what its feeble cascades
were still whispering
about Europe's formative years.

Then it was time to go in to the long tables
and the white cloths like fresh pages
waiting our clumsy portrayals
of two more 'dear British guests'.
O tour reps on mopeds,
who pass each other at sunset:
like lemon juice writing held over a lamp

each new drink spilt on the linen
made the script of the evening clearer!
I didn't want to be yelled at to drink more:
I wanted to know if the young Cretan men
the leaflet called 'proud and graceful'
were making up rude rhyming couplets
or singing 'Love is destined to break in two'
or 'When a man is born a grief is born'.

And there were so many songs
the young men could have been singing
to the long series of notes wandering
restlessly, anxiously, roads without end.
Songs praising various cities,
their women and their wine
or damning various cities, their women and their wine.
Songs which sing of small sorrows,
songs about Charon and Hades
and songs about mothers.
Songs which say 'You are like the sea
and you drown me', which say
'I don't fear death—only hunger'
or 'Night, you are the colour of the dress
my mother will wear when they bury me'.

The lights strung across the courtyard
shuddered in a chilly draught gusting down the hillside.
A bulb fell and smashed between the tables,
a woman screamed then laughed,
and one cold raindrop pricked my skin.

And then one of our party
was laid out by too much retsina.
Honour was satisfied and we were free to go.
On the way back, our reps roused us to song.

The drunk, dumped snoring in the aisle,
was possessed by the spirit of Elvis.
Miraculously resurrected, he lurched forward,
grabbed the driver's mike
and crooned 'Love Me Tender'
and 'Always On My Mind'.

The flickering tombs were behind us
and the Bishop's windows were dark;
and the headlamps and dim interior of the bus
were the only lights moving in that place.

The Graves

Dr. Kennedy's Country Dream

I dream of the Mower
    Twisting like smoke,
Withering and kindling,
    Consumed and uttered
In the field's haze.
    His doing is undoing;
He in unmaking makes.
    He inquires into tangled plots:
He is an *Alexander*
    To *Flora's* fragrant knots.
Under the arc of his scythe
    The whole Earth lies simplified.

I dream of the Mower,
    Disclosed from the heat's maze
Where *Flora* softly hums.
    The Mower holds my gaze
And ever closer comes.
    He spares none among the graves
And renders every spire of grass
    Into its own epitaph.
The bindweeds winding from my rot
    Are my eternity.
The Mower bends to read my stone
    And makes short work of me.

Books of the Dead

I

I remember writing
'things die and become books'
in a poem about Crete
without understanding it.
I remember the words
remaining irreducible
beyond a dim sense
of mess made into destiny,
of bustle grasped so made inert;
beyond a dim sense
of the poem itself
as dim sense miscarrying
the sound of the sun
hammering the sea.
Now I am thinking
of the dead letter office
with Rimbaud, Spicer and the others
all stacked up.

II

Everyone we meet
writes something in us
and we in them.
We leave our words
in each other,
maybe just a cadence
or a stress,
even an aspect of a style
to return unexpectedly,
quite likely unknown at first.
And we go on
walking and talking
into our lives,
already inflected.

III

Books of the dead:
rememberance books,
probate registers,
anthologies for dead poets.
Books of the dead:
our own address books,
the number of crossed-out
names recording
our own growing older,
our own diminishment.

IV

If there is an afterlife
it will be the long, dull ache
of a coach between cities,
the radio perhaps too loud
and the driver having to be asked
to put the air blowers on.
It will be reading
and, now and then,
snapping out of reading
to check the time and the timetable,
or look at stands of cows
or acid yellow rape fields
or the curious sheds
in the middle of nowhere
leaking posts and planks
under broken shutter doors,
and then turning back to reading
and the middle of the journey.

At Anton Walbrook's Grave

Winter microphones,
    Dead heads crackle in the grip,
Catch what sound there is
    To be tapped from the hard air
That sharpens the lines
    Of angel and obelisk,
And confirms the few stripped trees
    Mixed in with the evergreens
As bony fossils raised on crowded ground.

St. John's, by Hampstead,
    Resting two crafts, stage and state,
Kay Kendall, Gaitskell,
    Herbert Beerbohm Tree, squeezed you
Into its constraint.
    Fame's not a plant that grows on
Mortal soil, it's true, but here
    Celebrity's contraction
Seems much too crudely, and too amply, shown.

All your keenest roles,
    Anton, were keyed to music,
Dance and sex, three forms
    Where breathing, pulse and rhythm
Quicken and grow short,
    Rest a moment, then start up
Again and, from their cycling,
    Larger patterns gather;
As | *The Blue Danube* spins its sparkling strains |

From phrases that rise
    Then fall away. | A vision
Of intellectual
    Life | lit up by more worldly
Appetites, | you shone

Like a torch into the tomb |
Where England had gone to earth
    Too soon; | your moustache, | demi
Tasse, | set the dash | on your | panache. | Rest well,

Articulate shade
    Of an emotional style
Whose charming manners,
    Zest and wit are fancy dress
Or a straitjacket,
    Too carefully through-composed
Or boringly consistent,
    And, whatever, such hard work
To our facetiously brutal age.

Now, as the last light
    Draining from St John's stark isle
Hangs for a minute
    In the narrow ducts of day
And night's connecting
    Vessels, Anton's shade rises,
Speaking, pointing eye and mind
    To focus on the stripped trees'
Inky corals clutching the evening star:

"See how cunningly
    They script a double lesson
In daylight's margin!
    They rehearse our ending, yes?
Reduced to thin, stiff
    Imitations of ourselves;
Sleeping stems like those beneath,
    Frames empty of the warm, soft
Rigmarole that makes all of our knowing

And unknowing selves—"
    But the trees aren't stopped, I say;
Endlessly ending,
    They never end but go on
Arriving, cycling
    To the same pause, expecting
The redeeming syllables
    Of next year's whispering leaves.
That's not us—our cycling's harder to plot

And it has a stop.
    The first breath of night blows in
And Anton gutters,
    His words coming and going:
"Perhaps and perhaps . . .
Read, then, yearly reminders
    Of our uncompleted state,
Of life as hunger for form,
    Like partial music, or bewildered love."

My Father's Deaths

My father, dying, didn't tell us
he was going to pass the time learning a new language.
He just started talking like people in phrasebooks do,
with a skewed sense of proportion,
frightfully certain
about things of little or no consequence.
'This tea is too hot', he would say too loudly
or 'This water is far too cold'.

My father, dying, simplified his mind
until it was so thin
it was able to pass through its own bars
and escape.

My father, dying, was a room
full of deep snow pocked
with footprints that suddenly stopped
so no one knew where they went.

My father, dying, was neither an ocean liner at night
nor the paper streamers falling from it into the water
and still held in the hands of the people
waving goodbye from the dock
but just its wake
left on the water a long time.

My father, dying, was a hole
made by a railway ticket nipper
in a ticket that didn't exist
and all the members of the on-train team
gathered round but none of them knew
if they were supposed to be looking at the hole
or at the space where the ticket should have been

My father, dying, was a piece of my unbroken skin
where a healed scar appeared
which scabbed over then opened,
stitch by stitch, to a raw, fresh wound.

My father, dying, was a commentary
on a text that no longer existed
or, some scholars argued,
had never been written.

My father, dying, was a locked glass case
that neither of us had the key for
containing my life's work to date:
the scrawled and battered bundles
of the manuscript of a book of questions.

My father, dying, was a page
where all the letters slipped
to the bottom and lay in a heap
mumbling and whispering
and then dropped off.

Egyptian Elegy for My Father

for the 25th anniversary of his death, 16 April 2006

I — I SPEAK A BOOK OF BREATHINGS

The stiff, bare frames of trees
surface from fields of dissolving night
or shivery stacks of mist
clarifying into first light.

Under their empty leads, snowdrops,
crocuses, then daffs and bluebells
piece the sentences of Spring
into a new recension.

With each new year that begins to breathe
more easily, with so much working
to stay undeceived, you're harder
and harder to establish, Dad.

I have been doing the wrong work, scraping
carelessness and ignorance to the quick
again and again and then again,
keeping the archives raw;

so these are the wrong words again,
already stillborn as a letter,
a windy etcetera, a justification
instead of a poem.

Let the wrong words dissolve
in shivery mists of grief;
then, let the mists condense into absolute love.
In a clarified morning, I pick stones,

stack them in the fields' corners,
rake to a fine tilth and sow tears
to bring forth the flowers of right and truth
—even plain poppies or Love in a Mist,

any blooms that grow in ordinary soil,
would say this is the right work.
The stiff, bare frames of pride
rusting above sour, inactive fields

become poles for new growth,
the pergola of pink climbing roses
in my childhood garden,
gateway to mysteries of fruit,

a buzzy apse of plum,
thickets of gooseberry and currant
and wide plains lined with long green tents
of runner beans behind them.

I bind these unconditional lines
drawn from ancient beliefs
that cleansed, uncorrupted flesh
germinates a spiritual body

into a book of breathings.
With white-gloved hands I turn for you
its fragile pages of ironed out upset,
reset fracture, careful culture.

I offer you these words
to set you free of myself,
the maze of my wounded self-love.
I offer you these words

to let you stand as you were.
I have been waiting here so long
to offer you these words.
I clip the corner of one page

and make your ticket
into the space of speculation.

II — My Father Speaks 'The Poem at the Door'

All these must be known:
  I stop, therefore, and answer.
I speak the truth:
  The sun is rising.

The bolts of this door?
  The letters of my name dispersed
  into right and truth.
The right lintel of this door?
  My deeds weighed
  and ranked in the tables.
The left lintel of this door?
  My years restrung
  and tuned to my best days.
The fastening of this door?
  The unpronounceable
  skeleton of my roots.
The socket of the fastening?
  The unforeseeable
  branches of my growth.
The threshold of this door?
  The names of my son
  who writes, who hears, who grows.

My truth is spoken:
  The sun is risen.
All these are known:
  I pass on, therefore, by them.

III — I SPEAK THE POEM OF RELEASE 'THROUGH THE PLAINS TO THE HORIZON'

From fields of grasshoppers, O my father,
set out for the horizon, set out
through the plains of flooding rivers
where Ra's divine sailors bathe nightly
and daily and where the lags and lulls
of a long war were some of your times happiest.

> With writings on your tongue,
>   right words and true,
> you enter the horizon
>   on the beams of the great disk.

> Behind the doors
>   of the upper heavens, you pass;
> you see the utterances,
>   the ceremony of the work.

Stepping out into the yard, the night,
I pause: the air is toothless again
to say love is always possible, present, close.
I stare up and up into the stars:
they are the ends of countries, Dad, countries
of millions of years where you have your place.

Alum Raptures
i.m. Jack Beeching 1922–2001

I — A RENUNCIATIVE ARTIFICE

Turbid the chrism, my farded mascot,
a punnet of wind in her bessemer hair . . .
Spliced licks reconstruct,
from lexis down to deictics,
a period code:
poetry as agonist alembic;
the self hurt into utterance
and so making utterance hurt.
A renunciative artifice
where opacity and resistance
in seemingly steady lines
draw the reader into
performing meaning
as a struggle against
whatever normativities
she's internalised.

II — STAY BITTEN

A quarry takes a bite out of a hill:
economics' fierce desire
and the poet's own
to say the never said
and have it stay bitten
into language
via an isomorphous,
sweetish-sourish
register: emetic,
astringent or styptic.
Snake-hunter poet, stalking nouns,
adjectives his graspers.
Capture's metamorphosis:

unhanselled girl and *caponizing bomb*
strike like a vine or dry stick
stupid feet make viper. Few escape.

III — NAME YOUR OWN

Blurred borderlands
between surrealist, apocalyptic,
late romantic as in 'missed'
the last nightbus from Fitzrovia.
Negative-leaking names,
tagging excess at best
a fever treatable with etiquette;
at worst corrupt delusion.
Here is a strong stream
obscured not stopped
by rational poem-cities'
neat heritage, neater commerce.
Dip your kerchief, clean the blur:
rediscover excess as risk;
name your own 'main path',
your own 'way mislaid'.

IV — POST-MORTEM MANIFESTO: HOW TO WRITE POEMS

Rehearse your own last rites.
Flirt with mock.
Mode of speech: spasm.
Assume the muse is
a spin doctor sexing up dossiers.
Mystification hotter than the news.
Monosyllable weights on
fulcrums of *symbiotic doubletalk.*

Degrade the vigil.
Assume the muse is
a street recruiter for fascists
—raise your stick!
Crazy as a surd.
Move to the Med.
Food fight.
Live in what transfigures you.

V — THE AFTERPOEM

The afterpoem,
real and made-up mingled:
Beeching treats Malley
in a roaring pub.
This dream because
both poetries are like drinking,
getting God's clarity
via, say, Pieprzówka or Żubrówka,
risking one more
and one more until
one downs you.
Some die before they think,
says Jack. Says Ern:
I was a haphazard amorist
caught on the unlikely angles
of an awkward arrangement. Weren't you?

Six Staves for Koch's Grave

i.m. Kenneth Koch 1925–2002

1

One day the Nouns were clustered in the street
Outside the *Café Ça Va*, waiting for poets to hire them.
They stood in the gutter waving and shouting:
Fruit! Scarves! Necklaces! Not bad, I said,
    I *am* writing an elegy of sorts for Kenneth Koch, and laurels
And myrtles with their berries harsh and crude
    Are such inharmonious signs to mark his memory.
There'll be no angry grief—Koch's own lines
    Will tease me out of sadness. So, step forward,
Nouns intense and light enough to decorate his life and work.

2

Spring is in the trees! "It is time to garland
    a wonderful poet."
Spring! Nine red cranes are standing over the city
    This morning, eight for the months Persephone
Can spend with her mother and one for luck and you.
    And I'm with the city—I can't mourn you with black.
Instead, I'll call you dancer, numberless, bright impossible
    Musician, a book about the universe, though without you
The world will be as forlorn as the last Greek-speaking village
    In Anatolia, circa 1922. Now the cranes are moving
Their long arms, giving me and you their stiff red blessings.

3

In interviews, bad questions may hide the poet
Which nearly happened when I talked to you in Huddersfield
    In a sales reps' pit stop B&B and my stupid questions
About politics nearly flattened the freshly carbonated
        drink of you.
And in poetry, one poet may hide another poet:
Ashbery's indeterminate pronouns and O'Hara's walking
 —Which no-one ever says anything interesting about—
Keep distracting people from your poetry
    Which is, often, exactly what it looks like.
As Myers said, for you, the surface of a work is the work.

4

Look forward to always containing what is
Contained, you once wrote about a box, which seems
    To say: let's make the best of where and what we are.
Then there'll be good times and, possibly, good poems too
    To look back on. I think that is your great subject:
That, as we go on living and writing, living and writing
    Become kinds of elegies for their former selves
And that we go on resurrecting those selves
    In idealized landscapes to cope with the loss that comes
To us all because, after all, being is nearly all ebbing.

5

I remember, when I wrote the third stanza, remembering
Other things about August 5th 1993. I remember
    We were talking about a poet we both knew and you said,
"He just drinks and drinks all night until he folds in half
    Like a beautiful silk handkerchief." One of the loveliest
        things
I ever heard. I remember the heat upstairs at the venue
    And that when you asked the organizer of the reading
If there was somewhere you could go collect your thoughts
    He said, "Well, you could go and stand outside in the street".
Which is one of the rudest things I ever heard.

6

There is a way of thinking about happiness
But too many poets write as if poetry
    Isn't it and is a temple where happiness
Gets left outside with our shoes before we can go in.
    It's pretty crowded in there already—if the smell
From all those damp socks hasn't put us off!
    Thank you, Kenneth Koch, for showing us
Poems can be light like bossa novas and sambas;
    Or very simple or dumb—in a good way,
Like a production of Peter Pan; or fizzy

    Like a game of tennis with a beautiful girl.
Thank you, for showing us poems
    Don't have to be like those moments
Towards the ends of some late romantic symphonies
    When the composer has dragged us to the top
Of the most difficult alp in the great massif
    He has made out of his life and the music stops
To look out over infinity.

Postcards of Penthesilea
i.m. Nicholas Zurbrugg 1947–2001

When night falls, the traveller
   has given up trying
      to understand Penthesilea,

whether it exists or whether
   it 'is only the outskirts of itself',
      Marco Polo tells Kublai Khan.

Calvino's Venetian steps from
   your lovely phrase 'à fin
      de siècle Marco Polo'

to string the last century
   with exploration and evoke,
      distantly shimmering

between oases of talks,
   fugitive papers, listservs,
      the avant-garde's

own invisible cities,
   its projected worlds
      and projected citizenships.

In your mind and on your pages,
   we were already there,
      the horizon rolling back

like an intricate carpet
   to the salon of Orlan
      and Ned Zedd

where Acker yakkers
   with Stelarc about metabodies
      tattooed, sexed.

categories leak
　　disco-dada
it's how they do what they are
　　videopoesia sonora
spill possibility
　　writers as impatient readers
spill complexity
　　philosophers as failed artists
and the inverse is obvious
　　cut down cut in cut up

your sixteen letters
　　leak so many things
we saw you were
　　leak 'gush' spill 'grin'
as in fan as critic as fan
　　spill 'linch' as in pin
as in hyphen visions
　　future in a prefix
inter poly multi extra
　　cut in cut up cut down

from your names
　　we mine 'curb'
and remember
　　your hyphens splicing
dreams of futures past
　　to dv and mix
to show us art
　　has no power
to exclude only widen
　　cut up cut down cut in

your names leak 'grains'
    as in becoming forms
your sense of limit risked
    that swing between then out
where art dreams after
    us beyond us
where most reward's in movement
    take a car ride
down an unfinished road
    cut in cut up cut down

now you are thought
    in the heads of everyone
you met now you are code
    on the net your thoughts
html'd and uploaded
    into that perpetual present
we print you off and the date's
    always the day before tomorrow
yearning for the future
    cut down cut in cut up

now you are (your term)
    'the techno-t me'
my lines must leak you
    dynamic referent
my lines must leak you
    who saw words installed
saw words as ligne de base
    or point de depart
for echo and fragmentation
    cut up cut down cut in

categories leak
    it's how you are
now you are extra
    set on no one site
so no one site sets
    your becoming form/s
now you are
    an unfinished road
the long history of edge
    dreaming beyond us

        ⸌≈⸍

Zany animateur,
        it's our work now to stay logged on
            to Zurbrugg blog

and not just have a ball
        watching techno-bards Ballard
            and Baudrillard

tag the technopolis
        with 'end of days' wildstyle
            but keep the threads running,

sound and chart the currents
        of the counter-motion,
            plot the geometry beneath

the global multi-avant's fractals
        and keep faith with your faith
            that the arts you loved

and loved to link might,
    through being linked, build up
       into something more

than the Weltschmerz
    of endless outskirts,
       more than in Polo's words,

'a soupy city diluted in the plain.'
    You cannot take us any further,
       say 'Over here' or 'Nearly there',

but your sense that it's all right
    and possible to imagine remains.
       That is our gate, our way forward.

tag: a graffiti writer's signature; to leave one's signature.

wildstyle: a graffiti writing style using a complicated construction of inter-locking letters.

Poem Begun in a Small Notebook
i.m. Richard Caddel, poet & editor, 1949–2003

I

small talk
of the house
at night

after lights
out, day's
clinker—

floor surds,
pipe chortles,
fricatives

settlings
or wakings
in pathways

we barely know
as ins and outs,
ons and offs

our early insights
untransformed—
how easy

that is
and how we
hug it

unknowing
overlooking
as just reward

so each night's
day's done
and shutdown

is sleep
within
sleep

II

small talk
of the house
at night

dust
in the ear
shaping

our tenancy
of silence
and privacy—

we make it
and it
makes us,

returns
our being here
to us

Ric, we met
only in e-mails
but you were

still are
a presence
of care

a measure—
that we should
inhabit

the exact
weight of each breath
fully

and press on the world
at least
no more harm

Call & Response

Singers, singers,
    Where are you singing?
In all that we leave you
The dead love the living.

Singers, singers,
    How shall we hear you?
By sounding our words
And making them new.

History of the Woe

graciñas a Erín Moure

Who appears?

Who appears?

Who appears?

The Larks

Advice To All Girls In Love

You can never tell what the Atlantic will do next.
Too much monotony is bad for anyone.
What is the word we write most often
in our chequebooks? Isn't it 'Self'?

Shipboard is a dangerous environment.
Husbands are inclined to be sleepy.
All through history there have been such dark pages
when blushes were the fashion instead of cocktails

and the equality of the sexes. Can you play
second fiddle? Sometimes sworn enemies
bury their hatchet in the most surprising way.

A locked five-barred gate at the end of a pleasant walk,
thank Heaven, has gone out with chaperones and crinolines.
Why do you think people give parties at all?

Bohemian Fantasy

after Rimbaud's 'Ma Bohème'

Muse, fuck those corduroyed pretenders
straining bookworm heads through the skylights
of their career path, *pied-à-terre* attics, trying
to kiss your arse that way—look at me!

I'm already out here under your big skies,
clocking frequent guest bonus points
at the sign of the Big Dipper. Rhymes
I pick where I find them—shot streetlamps,

chip supper carcases—and where I spit
a forest of sonnets shoots up. Night comes on,
the first drop of dew falls straight into my brain like acid.

Then the stars come close and whisper to me
and the wind strums the sinews stretched tight
over my ribs. I curl up like a baby in its lullaby.

Chef in the Dusk

chef in the dusk chef in the dusk
    I repeat you
chef in the dusk chef in the dusk
dusk chef dusk chef
day night merge fly apart
    in chef's dusk   ·
day night merge fly apart
    in dusk chef
    in your night day
        day night
        night day
    escher chequer trousers
    in your day night
        night day
    escher chequer
        chef's dusk trousers
chef in the dusk chef in the dusk
    dusk dusted

Found on a Flipchart

The world is open for business
and you have the key chipped to scan
today's careful balance between
core brand and local offering
as you step up to the plate repping
your rep in three or four keywords
to major franchise partners use
while among rather than whilst
amongst and feelings should always
be in figures e.g. 3 percent
allow yourself free rein to bid
up your expectations he won't
know what speed you like what pressure
and in what order so get him
to watch put his hand over yours
so he can feel what you're doing
you will need to act quickly as
it can take three to five years
to develop a population
show your pleasure when he gets it
right look over there a skills gap
analysis in an undershopped
but affluent market without
moving your lips or acquiring
the right tools to identify
overtraining remember one
brand wardrobes no longer exist
past decade low fidelity
levels increased participation
for killers labour intensive
cut is outsourced keep these up
unfortunately this payment option
cannot be offered to share fishermen

Fabula Rasa

Challenge any two adults
to make the limits
of narrative
and they will point
to 'quiet zone'
'parts department'
infinite graphics
of women changing
infants which either
signal future hopes
or restate fixed roles

If you cannot find
or back engineer
your reservation
this is due to stock
formation problems
in chilled techno talk
there is space under
your seat for small soft
pamphlets full of ardour
but only if you have
language or your tongue
in your pocket

Ink Tunes

I

thought core
    dictation kiss

II

ingress trumpet
         probe tip
    said so

III

siege text
    touch tumble supplement

Art Texts — 1

HERITAGE PROJECT - 1

Make a raised flowerbed approximately 7 feet by 5 feet; and plant it with grass seed. Place a supermarket trolley on its side on the raised flowerbed. Let the grass grow as tall as possible until the supermarket trolley is either completely hidden or largely unrecognizable. Then carefully remove the grass and return the trolley to its original condition and an upright state. Place a plaque describing the project in front of the raised flowerbed.

HERITAGE PROJECT - 2

Visit as many heritage sites as possible. Collect the food and drink merchandise on sale. For example: The Duchess of Devonshire's Original Chocolate Chip Cookies or Anne Hathaway Tea. Make a very large collection. Donate the collection to a museum or gallery.

Lament of the River

after Laforgue

The narrow boats have gone the way
   Of yesterday's dog-day morning.
And there is a part of me
    That has gone with them forever,
     O gun carriage cortèges
     Of all my dead princesses!

So many things unravel me
  —Autumns, TV agony shows—
I might as well be sixteen again!
    I'm just the niggling jingle
     Of keys in my pocket
     —Keys that don't fit anyone's locket.

So I walk and sit, sit and walk,
    Without direction, without imagination.
My heart was buried on an island
    In a lake long before I was born.
     It'll never be my turn to tryst
     In Happiness's waiting list.

My Dream Tom Raworth's Oklahoma Windows

I come down to make breakfast on Sunday morning and find Tom Raworth in our kitchen. He is assembling a large white cardboard construction. It is in the form of a tall, thin triangle and printed with text and black abstract designs. He explains that all the shapes and tabs have been cut by hand and we agree that is much cheaper than paying for a cutting forme.

Then he explains he must leave as he is late for another project in Oklahoma. He shows me a small stained glass window. It is half moon shaped with a lateral section at the bottom and three pieces in a fan shape on the curved edge. The middle one is in blood red glass; the others are a milky, off-white colour. The words 'Apollo Apollo' are printed across the surface.

When my wife comes down and I tell her about Tom Raworth's visit she already knows all about it. The window is part of a project for the Oklahoma Bus Company and the actual name is 'Lollo Apollo'.

My Dream Alan Halsey's Sentences Cool Down

He is about to read, fatter than in real life and dressed in jeans and a short-sleeved shirt instead of his usual dapper suit. He greets the audience and then turns his back to them.

After a minute or so his head turns round to face them. He speaks: "I'm interested by the way that the further we get from Christianity sentences cool down but remain charged."

My Dream Frances Presley Delivers A Book

I am waiting for a book to arrive from Peter Riley. There is a knock at the door. Expecting the postman I am astonished to see Frances Presley. She has a large shoulder bag like a postman and is dressed in a tight-fitting navy uniform. She explains she has taken over Peter Riley's business and is delivering all orders personally. She looks about ten years younger and has the toned figure of a teenage girl.

My Dream Picasso Shows Me The Secret

I meet the young Picasso
and he offers to show me The Secret.

He asks me for a clean piece of paper.
He doodles something in the centre.

Then, at the top, he writes 'Femininity';
and, at the bottom, 'Innocence'.

Myth in Samoa

A language instructor was explaining
a process of leaning to arouse your partner.
"A myth in Samoa is a rare event

and a fun time with no consequences.
You can interact with live women
who are eager to talk to you personally

like a box of chocolates,
the pre-eminent form of bringing love
into physical reality."

Is your brain like a box of chocolates?
Details of day to day rules and routines
when you lose your head are relatively easy.

Loving is zero usually at home,
more than a three-letter word
and loaded with assumption.

The secret of a young woman's business success
is a normal and healthy part of our lives,
a killer wireless application,

and god's joke on human beings.
Keeping her slim is a religious experience.
The multi-dimensional nature

of true humanity is necessary, proper and costly.
A stab in the dark for an octopus is optional.
Anger is making me too like a typewriter.

Poem

'Prosody is all Greek to most people . . .'
PETER SANSOM

This is the poem inflatable beds
make for me off Pefkos beach Pefkos beach

This is the poem blue orange blue green
silver pink beryl they make me in Crete

Blue purple toffee yellow chartreuse jade
oxblood green grey cobalt green grey old gold

White silver blue yellow red purple pink
this is the poem now let's get a drink

Art Texts — 2

Film Project

Collect footage from CCTV cameras showing deserted urban spaces — e.g. car parks — at night. Montage these together so that there is a slow, classical rhythm. Make a soundtrack from film noir music. Project the finished footage in front of urban CCTV cameras.

Seven Deadly Sins

Collect seven cigarette butts. Arrange the butts so that they spell the word 'sin'. Photograph in large format and exhibit.

Symphonie Fantastique
after Rimbaud's 'À la musique'

Struggling like insects drowning in droplets
of August's marmalade, the bourgeoisie spread
their fat arses on thin slices of bench in the poxy square
where everything's laid out like a 'just so' story.

A band hasn't played here for forty years
but crusty captains of huge desks tow their bloated wives
round and round the bandstand in memory of it.
Single women parade themselves like walking billboards

in front of single men pretending to sneer at their mobiles.
Two old guys in blazers put the world to rights,
involuntarily stiffening to attention every few minutes
at the call of some haunting, interior bugle.

I'm dressed like a street person in greasy clothes
too warm for this weather and, like every Saturday,
I let the married men stalk me under the chestnut trees,
fingering their rings as their eyes fill with indiscreet things.

I do not say a word: I let them keep looking
at the flash of my white neck embroidered with stray locks:
I take off my parka and they follow, under my t-shirt,
the divine back below the curve of my shoulders.

Soon one has taken me to the roofless redbrick Gents
behind the yew hedge. His fierce desires fasten on to my
      crotch . . .
There is no time and no need to speak together in low voices.
Hands behind my head, I look up into the afternoon heat

and watch the thin clouds unravel like milk in water . . .

Teach Yourself Criticism: The Texas Poetry Examiner

During one somewhat lively decade of an otherwise prosaic life, I worked the Rio Buffalo as a US Poetics Patrolman, and every night I wished for just such a fine volume as this big bruiser, this fine new howitzer, [INSERT BOOK TITLE]. Sometimes during an eight-hour shift we had as many as three separate and distinct controversies. Had this big volume been around, what a lulu of a pacifier it would have been.

This [INSERT BOOK TITLE] is a man's book. It ain't for boys. Word has reached me that some Joes, probably with lace on their panties, are wearing gloves to read it. I have heard that after a few pages your hand feels like you have been swinging at some fast balls with a cracked bat. How soft can we get? I read [INSERT BOOK TITLE] all one afternoon and found the recoil nothing more than stimulating. The kick kind of reminds me of the existing situation down in Dixie where a certain clientele now buy their white lightnin' over the liquor counter in preference to the smoother and legitimate bourbon. Asked why, they explain it's for the kick. Me, I'm the same way about [INSERT BOOK TITLE].

Sure, it kicks. But not hard enough to hurt your hand; not enough, certainly, to remove any hide. That's for the birds. The recoil is a heart-warming, exhilarating sort of thing. Something like standing behind one of these Nike ground-to-air missiles and setting 'er off with your own two sweaty little hands. You feel like you have really done something. I like to read the book. I'm betting you will, too.

The Return of the Art of Poetry

Where would we be without the Pyramids
or the Eiffel Tower? The Pyramids

and the Eiffel Tower follow very strict
structural guidelines. The Pyramids

are examples of traditional structures
that were repeated for thousands of years.

The Eiffel Tower was based on sound
engineering principles—if it wasn't

it would fall down. The same is true
for poetry. Poets who turn their backs

on thousands of years of experiment
with form do themselves a disservice.

Strict form sometimes makes language just glow.
It is great to see that you are looking

at how you write though as that is the mark
of a good writer. I also feel that

the older forms of writing such as
crossword puzzles are making a comeback.

The Wild Anger is Tired of Soap

She is late,
dropping her body.
He can hear her flesh
—she knows that for a streetlight.

'You're late,' he say.
'You've dropped
your body,' he says.

Somewhere,
there is a wild anger
tired of soap.
The last few months
have had a twinge
of the door.

Suddenly,
he walks back
to his forehead,
to his stomach.

She unfastens her door
until he cranes his breath.
She steps around the kitchen
and into his ears.

Her eyes
are a brilliant idea.

When there is no more beer,
he pulls her head.

What To Eat in Poland, or, We Say What We See
for Elżbieta Wójcik-Leese

I

We say what we see. Middle class roast. Smoked eel who likes to swim in pepper sauce. Yellow and green desire cream. The translator is sometimes forced to resort to compensation strategies.

II

The Polish printer had changed 'real' to 'read' and when I corrected this mischievous Magda said, "O, you've put mushrooms in the poem" and explained that the word for 'mushroom' means literally 'the real thing'.

III

"At Easter, we have white borscht and special little dumplings. This year my mother and grandmother made 150; but you can't do it just for yourself."

IV

One year later, and Jacek tells me the mushrooms would have to be the species called 'prawdziwek'. The root word is 'prawda'—'truth'—so 'prawdziwek' might also mean 'something truthful' but with the implication of being small. This is a nice word, like when you say Willie instead of William. So: 'prawdziwek': something (but also 'someone' is possible) truthful and reliable, containing truth, something (or someone) rather small. And rather nice.

V

Road's endless seam across the central plain. Roadside stands selling apples from crates arranged in vertical chequerboards. Red orange russet green. May can't be the right time of year for apples. We say what we see.

WARSAW — ŁÓDŹ — WARSAW, MAY 2003

When I Was Spanish

I

The waters were cold.
The souls of men were immortal.
There were fewer people and more conveniences.
There were as many men as women.

II

Women loved flowers.
Horses were strong.
Dogs were useful.
The children washed their faces.
Mexico had more inhabitants than Argentina.

III

My brother liked the lawyer,
but he did not like the physician.
We closed the window.
We counted the books.
We scoured the pans.
We slept little.
I never passed such nights.

IV

You were hungry.
What a handsome horse you had!
I gave you my watch for your bicycle.
You came with me to the bank to identify me.

V

There was a good furnace in the basement of my father's house.
He talked of nothing but Montevideo.
He did not give you the chairs: he did not give them to you.
He was buying iron with gold.
He said that he could not warm the house with flowers.
He went out through the window.

VI

I liked perfumes,
but I preferred taste to the sense of smell.
I looked for my parents.
I wished I could wear a duck suit
and white canvas shoes
while we were crossing the plains.

Word Girl

after Rimbaud's 'Au Cabaret Vert'

The barmaid was Venus after just one swallow
of the hobo's traditional all day breakfast:
a jug of amber, the falling sun's last resting place.

That grail on tap had kept me sliding
and scrambling in torn jeans and busted boots
down trails and clefts as steep but not as kind

as the one between her massive tits where sweat beaded
and ran, warping and blurring the words printing
and scrolling there. That's why I was trying to peer

down her front. She saw me looking and smiled
like *I* was a book and she'd guessed the ending
on p.1. Between her white teeth I glimpsed

her small pink tongue. I thought about it all the time
I ate the chilled ham she brought and the few potatoes
still warm from lunch. Yes, it was around five in the afternoon

when I stopped and looked down into the city,
fitful in a blue fog of erotic daydreams about itself;
and I didn't realise how much I'd lost the plot

till I stretched out my legs in the Cabaret Vert.

Art Texts—3

MONEY

Obtain a brand new £50 note. Mount on card and frame expensively. Dimensions 4ft long by 2ft high. Exhibit for sale at £500 or £5000 depending on gallery and what you think you can get away with.

MORE OR LESS

Buy a plain white t-shirt. Screenprint as follows: on the front 'More Art'; on the back 'Less Art'. Colour optional. Wear to any art event you attend.

Cornell: A Circuition Around His Circumambulation

The boxes seem like machines. They hark back to entertainment machines of a bygone age: nickelodeons, 'what the butler saw', penny-in-the-slot machines. 'Hark': 'to listen to' but also 'to pay close attention to'. 'Hark back': 'to retrace a course until a scent is regained'; 'to turn back to an earlier topic or circumstance'; 'to go back to something as an origin or source'. The boxes hark back and so the viewer harks back. The boxes seem like machines. More specifically they reveal a set of what appear to be working parts. The mind's first questions are always 'what is the motor?' and 'what is the sequence?' and each time one of the boxes is viewed a different set of answers or relationships offers itself. It might be the case that each box contains the parts of or the operating instructions for a whole set of machines, in conjunction with all the other boxes. And like those entertainment machines of a bygone age, the boxes promise the possibility that if those questions can be answered definitively or perhaps just asked in the right way something mysterious might be revealed—but, of course, it never is. So the fascination and reward of each work is the perpetual repetition or restaging of this tension between revelation and conceal-ment. They are like magic tricks, grand illusions, but they are also magical. There is something in the boxes' portability that makes them talismanic. They are time machines. Boxes for trav-elling great distances without moving.

|2|

Peter mails from 'down under' to say: 'I saw the Cornell show at the Whitechapel Gallery on my way home to Brixton the morning after the riots, so to go from that to burnt out shops and strange quietness merely fixed him in my heart.' And this seems just right in so many ways, in objects and elements that combine in so many ways. Cornell. A journey across a city. Memory. Sudden change in a city. The past. Strange quietness. Other walkers. Other walks. The human heart. Cornell.

[3]

The boxes hark back to entertainment machines of a bygone age: nickelodeons, 'what the butler saw', penny-in-the-slot machines. And this, in turn, evokes the places of childhood: the fair, seaside holidays. Cornell made many of the boxes as amusements for his brother Robert. In an essay on Cornell published in *Art News* in 1967, John Ashbery wrote that, 'The genius of Cornell is that he sees and enables us to see with the eyes of childhood, before our vision got clouded by experience, when objects like a rubber ball or a pocket mirror seemed charged with meaning, and a marble rolling across a wooden floor could be as portentous as a passing comet.'

Cornell is strolling. He must be the only person alive who knows that faded picture of a ballerina is a key to a lost structure of feeling. Guy Debord wrote in *The Society of the Spectacle*: 'Everything that was directly lived has moved away into representation.' The boxes evoke shop window displays. In *Window Shopping: Cinema and the Postmodern*, Anne Friedberg writes of the advent of glass shop windows: 'Objects placed behind glass were altered (and in some cases improved) in their appearance.' The boxes evoke shop window displays and perhaps also the arcades or 'passages' of an earlier age. Cornell is walking in the opposite direction to everyone else. Anne Friedberg writes of Walter Benjamin's uncompleted *Passagen-Werk*, a study of the Paris arcades: 'Benjamin took the "passages" as a succinct instantiation of the fragmentary nature of modernity [. . .] The passage (and here it is important to retain the word *passage*—not arcade) was an architectural monument to *time* and its passing.' She goes on to quote Adorno describing Benjamin's method: '[He was] drawn [. . .] to everything that has slipped through the conventional conceptual net or to things which have been esteemed too trivial by the prevailing spirit for it to have left any traces other than those of hasty judgement.' Adorno continues: 'He was drawn to the petrified, frozen or obsolete elements of civilization, to everything in it devoid of domestic vitality no less irresistibly than is the collector to fossils or to the plant in the herbarium. Small glass balls containing a landscape upon which snow fell when shook were among his favourite objects.' In March 1926, Benjamin went to Paris to work with Franz Hessel on a joint translation of Proust's *Remembrance of Things Past*. Anne Friedberg writes 'For both Benjamin and Hessel, city streets served as a mnemonic system, bringing images of the past into the present . . . ' and that for Benjamin the arcade or passage represented 'a spatial verse of visual display.'

[5]

The boxes evoke shop window displays, particularly those of second-hand or junk shops, which underlines that his art is profoundly urban but in a particular way. It makes a complex response to the city that is no longer possible because the city as Cornell knew it no longer exists. This is the city as an enormous material memory, a laying down of layer upon layer of *stuff*, a multi-layered sediment of dreams and passions and obsessions. Old loves. Bygones. Discarded tokens of sentimental educations. In such a city it was possible to be the archivist and reanimator not just of ancient desires but also of the forgotten taste of other ages. Cornell is strolling. He must be the only person alive who knows that faded picture of a ballerina is a key to a lost structure of feeling. In such a city it was possible to browse, to stroll, to potter, because the city had not yet become the site of brutally short boom-bust cycles of total refashioning. Cornell's city was expanding but was not then a place where factories became apartments, warehouses studios and banks became café bars. Cornell's New York was still a place of what a commentator of 1949 called 'historical piquancies'. Cornell's browsing and pottering seems relegated—at least in England— to old-fashioned seaside resorts like Whitstable or Swanage, itself made up of bits of old London from the sixteenth and seventeenth centuries salvaged by the builder John Mowlem in the mid-nineteenth century.

Debord

       Qui?

            Debord

                       C'est lui? Oui

Debord

            Debord

                     qui dérive

                     who drifts

        drifts away from   the subject
                                       (pun intended)

        Cornell

              circuits   Les jours de Joseph le jouisseur qui jouit

le jaja de jau

les joujoux de Joe   circulation

                   circumambulation
                constellation

circuition   (archaic): "the act of circuiting"
             (archaic): "a circuitous mode of reasoning or arguing"

             the distant chime with "intuition" suggests
             another meaning: "immediate apprehension by
             the mind without reasoning through walking
             the city like a meditation"

                Frank the flâneur

                          "his supposed lack of will"
                Frank qui flâne
                Frankie Flann
            The Further Adventures of Frankie Flann

                        O'Hara's ology
             bohobohara

ontology
the performance
ontogenesis
of non-performance

AMBLING ALPHABET *or* DRIFT DIRECTORY

[Towards a Meeting of Incongruous Walkers]

Aragon
Baudelaire
Calle
Debord
E
Fisher
G
H
I
Joyce
K
Laforgue
Mac Low
Nerval
O'Hara
Poe
Q
Reznikoff
Sinclair
T
U
V
W
X
Y
Z

There is something in the boxes' portability that makes them talismanic. There is too something of the ritual in the collection of materials, the waiting for the right moment to begin construction, and in the eventual construction. There is a Sherlock Holmes story called 'The Adventure of the Musgrave Ritual'. It begins with Holmes, at Watson's behest, tidying up his rooms and going through the relics of his early cases. He comes up with 'a small wooden box, with a sliding lid, such as children's toys are kept in. From within he produced a crumpled piece of paper, an old-fashioned brass key, a peg of wood with a ball of string attached to it, and three rusty old discs of metal.' The story revolves around an old aristocratic family and the ritual of the title which has been handed down from father to son since the middle of the seventeenth century. Holmes calls it a 'strange catechism' and part of it goes as follows: 'Whose was it? His who is gone. Who shall have it? He who will come. Where was the sun? Over the oak. Where was the shadow? Under the elm. [. . .] What shall we give for it? All that is ours. Why should we give it? For the sake of the trust.' The objects, the criminal relics, that Holmes has kept might very well form part of a Cornell box. We might well imagine a 'strange catechism' being attached to each box. And the boxes do also evoke the wayside shrines that are seen in such countries as Greece.

In *Count Zero*, the second novel in William Gibson's cyberspace trilogy, an Artificial Intelligence forges Cornell boxes. One of Gibson's characters imagines shop window displays are like Cornell boxes because, in both, objects and materials are 'arranged to suggest geometrics of nameless longing'. Cornell and cyberspace activate intriguing resonances. Gaston Bachelard, writing in *The Poetics of Space*, argued that 'inhabited space transcends geometrical space'. This describes our experience of the Internet, our experience of Cornell's boxes, Cornell's experience. The World Wide Web is possible because of Hypertext Markup Language (HTML), the computer code which allows a 'web page' to contain 'links' to other web sites. The physical residence of web sites is largely unknown to the viewer and is, indeed, unimportant. The objects and materials in a Cornell box are versions of these 'links' to places, to sites, whose physical existence remains mysterious. Melbourne-based artist Steven Goldate finds similarities between 'links' on 'web pages' and the 'plaque tournante' of the Situationists. He quotes Asger Jorn's comment that a 'plaque' can lead to 'spontaneous turns of direction taken by a subject moving through these surroundings in disregard of the useful connections that ordinarily govern his conduct.' The objects and materials in Cornell's boxes are the results of his activity as a flâneur, of his walking the city. Steven Goldate argues that we are all becoming cyberflâneurs in the informatic cities of the World Wide Web.

Cornell's boxes prefigure the way that history has got shorter. They predict the way that nostalgia for a very recent past became a key fact of late twentieth century thinking. Culture became memory. And because the boxes are always flickering somewhere between fascination and obsession, fandom and stalking, looking and voyeurism, they force us to ask questions about what nostalgia is, what history is. They force us to ask questions about the nature of desire. They are looks that can never be returned just as they fail to return our own looks to us.

Peter mails from 'down under' to say: 'I'm reminded of the walking that Guy Debord and his cronies used to do, though I can't remember what they called it.' La dérive. Théorie de la dérive. Dérive, *nf*, 'drift'. Dériver, *vi*, (*Aviat, Naut*), 'to drift'; (*fig*) [*orateur*] 'to wander' *ou* 'drift (away) from the subject'. From 'Théorie de la dérive': 'passage hâtif à travers des ambiances variées', 'effets de nature psychogéographique', 'un comportment ludique-constructif'. Comportment: behaviour, performance. 'Ludic' is another way of writing 'lucid'. Psychogeographical readings. Quick scans of different environments. The Situationists tried to construct situations that would disrupt the ordinary and the normal in order to jolt people out of their customary ways of thinking and acting. Instead of petrified life, they proposed the *dérive* with its flow of acts and encounters. Walking as resistance. Walking as refusal. 'Théorie de la dérive' was first published in December 1956. In Cornell's papers for that month, two typewritten notes. '12/20/56: non-diary.' '12/26/56: reminder. what about constellation for experiment in going over past experiences on various subjects and picking out certain points for a presentation.' Walking as resistance. Walking as refusal. Cornell walking against time and modernity. He is the only person alive who knows that faded picture of a ballerina is a key to a lost structure of feeling. He is walking in the opposite direction to everyone else.

He is not the poet. Perfecting it later. After a gap of time. Every day he does the best he is. The best he is is having no 'later', no 'gap'. He has really seen the famous ballerinas of yesteryear dancing in theatres that no longer exist. He has taken tea with them and shyly given them a box made in their honour. His is the life that can never be satisfactorily proved to have happened. He is not the poet. Perfecting it later. After a gap of time. Every day he does the best he is. The best he is is having no 'later', no 'gap'. This is how he counters the city. Its symbols of nothing. Its symbols of meaning of nothing. The city exists only as the archive of his own desires. So he walks it. He walks the same walks and finds the same things each time, literally the same things recreated each time for him. The boxes are records of walking, maps outside conventional time and space. They are monographs whose knowledge can only be known by walking. He is the one countering the city. Gathering records of his traces across it. He is the one always working too slowly. Left with traces of records of walks that can never be re-walked.

Notes

Another Moment: A Georgic . . . was written in response to John Kinsella's poem 'Moment in the sun: a georgic . . .' which was sent to the author in March 2003 and published in *The Australian* in May that year.

553 Steps Around Auzon. Auzon is a medieval town in the Haut-Allier area of the Auvergne, France.

Minster offers a series of textual remarks on masons' marks in Southwell Minster, Nottinghamshire. 'Masons' marks' is a term used to describe both personal marks left by medieval stonemasons and marks they used to indicate the positioning of stones.

The Process of Language. Special thanks are due to Peter Middleton for an extensive and pertinent critique of an earlier version.

Rehearsing Two of Ric Caddel's '5 Career Moves . . .' for a Reading. On Sunday, 19 October 2003 I participated in a reading organized by Ric Caddel's publisher West House Books, partly devoted to his posthumous collection *Writing in the Dark.*

Dhromi: The Roads. Dhromi, the plural of dhromos meaning literally 'road' and also used to denote the modal scales of traditional Greek song.

At Anton Walbrook's Grave. Anton Walbrook (1900–1967), born Adolph Anton Wilhelm Wohlbrueck, Viennese film actor best known for his roles as Stefan Radetzky, pianist and composer of the 'Warsaw Concerto', in *Dangerous Moonlight* (1941); the Svengali-like ballet impresario Lermontov in Powell and Pressburger's *The Red Shoes* (1948); and the Master of Ceremonies in Max Ophul's *La Ronde* (1950).

Egyptian Elegy for My Father incorporates material from E. A. Wallis Budge's 1899 translation of *The Egyptian Book of the Dead.*

Alum Raptures. Jack Beeching's poetry probably received its widest readership via *Penguin Modern Poets 16,* first published 1970. With the exception of the last three lines of section V taken from *The Darkening Ecliptic* by Ern Malley, the italicized words and phrases are taken from Beeching's poems in the Penguin volume. The reference in section IV to raising a stick against a fascist street recruiter refers to an encounter Beeching had in his early 70s with a recruiter for Jean-Marie Le Pen's National Front. Pieprzówka and Żubrówka are brands of Polish vodka, flavoured respectively with pepper and bison grass (*hierochloe odorata*).

Six Staves for Koch's Grave. Each section begins with a directly quoted or reworked opening line from one of Kenneth Koch's poems.

Postcards of Penthesilea includes quotations from Italo Calvino's *Invisible Cities* (Picador, 1979).

Advice to All Girls in Love uses material from *Between You and Me* by Ruby M. Ayres (Hodder & Stoughton, 1935).

Teach Yourself Criticism: The Texas Poetry Examiner adapts material from *The Pistol Shooter's Book* by Colonel Charles Askins (Collier Books, 1962).

What To Eat in Poland, or, We Say What We See. Thanks to Jacek Gutorow for the 'real truth' about mushrooms at the last minute.

When I Was Spanish adapts exercises in *Heath's First Spanish Course* (1918) by E. C. Hills and J. D. M. Ford.

Cornell: A Circuition Around His Circumambulation incorporates material from the following sources: e-mails from Peter Kenneally to the author, 16 January 2000; Anne Friedberg, *Window Shopping: Cinema and the Postmodern* (1993); John Gunther, *Inside USA* (1949); Glyn Maxwell, 'Dunn, Larkin and Decency', in *Reading Douglas Dunn* (1992); Peter Marshall, *Demanding the Impossible* (1992); and Joseph Cornell's *Theater of the Mind: Selected Diaries, Letters and Files* (1993).